From the Bedroom to the Barnyard

A Nine-Block Sampler Honoring Barn Quilts

by Kansas City Star Quilts

MW00638596

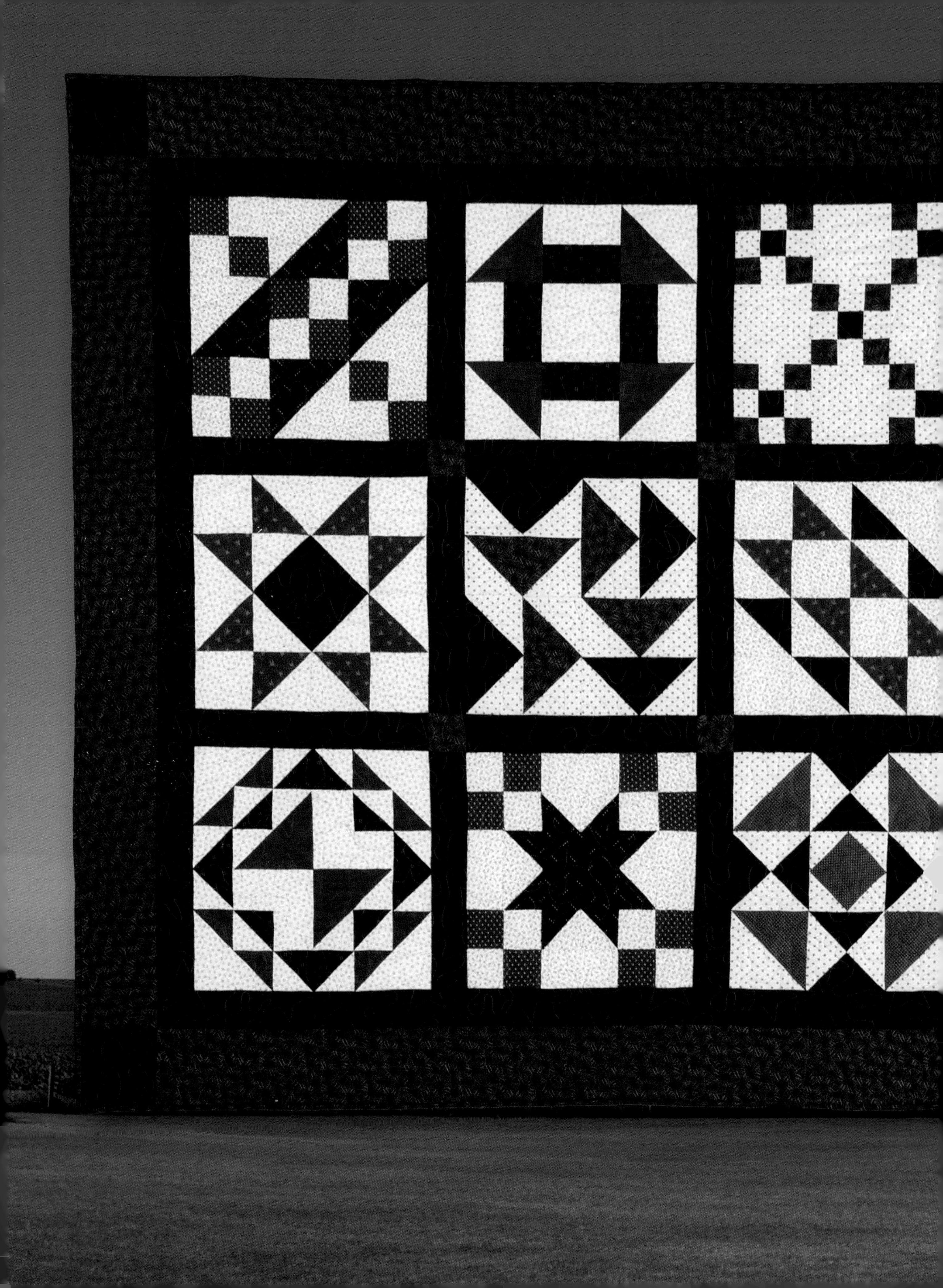

Barn Quilt Fabric Requirements

Size: 52" square

- 1 2/3 yards black and cream shirting fabrics
- 2 1/4 yards red – includes sashing squares, border and binding
- 2 1/4 yards blacks – includes sashing strips and inner border

We used 5 different reds, 4 blacks, and 3 black and cream shirtings. You may mix and match or use one fabric of each color. We're partial to using different fabrics for the interest and the movement achieved by doing so.

Editor: Doug Weaver
Quilting instructions: Edie McGinnis
Barn profiles: Doug Weaver
Designer: Kelly Ludwig
Photography: Aaron T. Leimkuehler, Kelly Ludwig, Doug Weaver
Illustration: Eric Sears
Technical Editor: Jane Miller
Production assistance: Jo Ann Groves

Published by:
Kansas City Star Books
1729 Grand Blvd.
Kansas City, Missouri, USA 64108
All rights reserved
Copyright © 2010 The Kansas City Star Co.

No part of this book may be reproduced, stored in a retrieval system, or transmitted in any form or by any means, electronic, mechanical, photocopying, recording or otherwise, without the prior consent of the publisher

First edition, first printing

ISBN: 978-1-935362-74-6

Printed in the United States of America by Walsworth Publishing Co., Marceline, MO

To order copies, call StarInfo at (816) 234-4636 and say "Books."

Acknowledgements

We owe a huge debt of gratitude to the following talented quilting friends for making blocks and testing the instructions for the quilt: Clara Diaz, Carol Christopher and Brenda Butcher of Independence, Mo., and Margaret Falen of Grain Valley, Mo. Brenda not only made blocks but is the talented quilter who quilted the quilt.

Thanks to Karlene Cooper for opening her home to the stitchers. She's the indispensable friend who pressed for everyone and ripped seams when someone made a mistake. Doris Heath sewed with us and offered moral support and a little humor when needed.

This book would have been impossible without the design and photography talents of Kelly Ludwig, the eagle eye of Jane Miller, the photo and production work of Aaron Leimkuehler and Jo Ann Groves, and the graphics help of Eric Sears.

Many thanks, too, to Diane McLendon, Kansas City Star Quilts' publisher, for her help and support.

We also thank the owners of the barns for the time they spent retelling their barns' histories and allowing us to take photographs.

And finally, a special thanks to Donna Sue Groves, founder of the barn-quilt movement; Suzi Parron, who chronicles its growth on her blog *Barn Quilts and the American Quilt Trail*; and Sue Peyton, who is the cheerleader for the amazing Sac County, Iowa, barn trail for their help in sharing the history of barn quilts.

- Doug Weaver and Edie McGinnis,
Kansas City Star Quilts

Contents

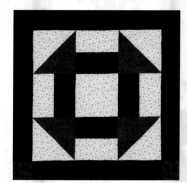

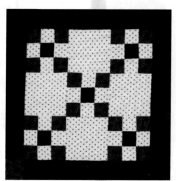

Introduction

If you stick only to the interstate rather than the nation's back roads, pity you. Because there, on many of America's rural highways, you will see an arts movement spreading across the country like, well, a home spun quilt.

Crest a two-lane road in Pennsylvania, Kentucky, Ohio, Iowa, Michigan, Illinois or California, or in any of 20 other states, and they will surely catch you by surprise: giant quilt blocks brightly painted in striking colors fixed tightly to the peaks or sides of barns, silos and other structures – beacons of warmth on the rolling hills and flat prairies of the nation.

The blocks have glorious names, some as rich in history as the weather-beaten barns they hang on: "Corn and Beans," "Illinois Star," "Amish Diamond," "Golden Wedding Ring."

Like quilting itself, the growth of barn-quilt "trails" is a grass-roots movement. There is no massive, single organization behind it. Sure, it has its pioneers and fervent supporters. But the barn-quilt fever is as much about satisfying a community's artistic itch as it is prettyin' up a barn.

"Did I think it'd grow to being in 27 states so fast, in 10 years?" asks Donna Sue Groves, the acknowledged founder of the barn-quilt movement. "No. I'm surprised, I'm thrilled. I'm so happy to hear from people about how they've met their neighbors ... how it's changed their lives."

Donna Sue's story set the stage for this cultural phenomenon. She and her mother, Nina Maxine Groves, purchased a small piece of property in 1989 in the foothills of Appalachia – in Adams County, Ohio. It included a dowdy gray tobacco barn. Donna Sue promised her mom, a long-time quilter from West Virginia, that some day she'd paint a quilt block on the barn to brighten it up.

It would take until 2003 for the block to actually happen, but an interesting thing evolved during those intervening years: Donna Sue grew more active in the local and state arts community. So when a friend offered to finally paint that quilt block for her, Donna Sue suggested instead that the entire county get in the act.

The idea was novel: Create a collection of barn quilts not just for their aesthetics but to help build community and drive tourism.

The county, plus the Ohio Arts Council and The Nature Conservancy, enthusiastically embraced the concept. And so was born the nation's first barn trail – the Adams County Quilt Barn Sampler project – featuring 20 barns, each symbolizing in its own way the joy of Appalachian culture.

The project was like a lit match in a field of parched grass. Word spread rapidly, and soon reports came in of barn-quilt movements in neighboring Ohio counties, but also in Tennessee, Iowa, North Carolina and West Virginia. And in Pennsylvania, Kentucky, Michigan and more. Donna Sue could track them all, because she'd be the first to get a call from hopeful organizers.

And her advice was always the same: Don't limit yourself to just what the folks in Adams County did.

"I'd tell them, 'There is no barn police,'" she said. "My premise from the very beginning was, once we created the model, other communities could take it and tweak it and change it, then share those ideas with others who follow."

And that's exactly what's happened. No two trails are alike. Travel to the Old Mission area of Michigan, and you'll see quilt blocks showcasing native cherries. Stop in at the massive trail in Sac County, Iowa, and you'll see the "Corn and Beans" block overlooking fields of, yes, corn and beans.

Perhaps the person most on top of the latest barn-quilt news is Suzi Parron, operator of a blog called *Barn Quilts and the American Trail* (americanquilttrail.blogspot.com) and author of an upcoming book by the same name, to be published by Ohio University Press.

Spin through Parron's blog and you'll sample the richness and geographic diversity of the barn-quilt movement. At the time I'm writing this, Suzi has news about the new California trail, the newest addition to the Kankakee quilt trail, a photo of a moose by a smallish quilt barn in Ontario (Canadian trails seem to be emerging!), the latest on the expansion of the Pennsylvania Grange quilt trail, and a photo of an incredibly crazy art-quilt block from a barn artist in Kentucky. And that's just the tip of it!

"I started it as a travel blog," Suzi said. "Now it's made up more of what people are sending me." She hopes eventually to create a single web site that would list all of the barn trails with links to their individual sites.

Given the enormity of the movement, this book seeks only to call more attention to the trails by featuring nine of our favorite barns and their quilt blocks. We've bundled the blocks into a barn-quilt sampler with all of the instruction needed to make the quilt. (Two of the blocks – "Railroad Crossing" and "Wild Goose Chase" – vary slightly from the barn blocks.) And we spent time visiting with the owners of each barn to learn its history.

Edie McGinnis, long-time Kansas City Star Quilts author and editor, created the quilt and provided the instructions. We also snapped quite a few photos on the road – "we" meaning myself and the book's designer, Kelly Ludwig. We chose to focus on the Old Mission Trail in upper Michigan, the Kankakee Trail in Illinois, and on our neighbors to the north, the grand Sac County Trail in Sac County, Iowa.

Finally, we have included a resource page with links to web sites of some of our favorite quilt-barn trails. While we tried very hard to include everyone, we don't claim this to be a comprehensive list. If we missed a trail here or there, we very much apologize.

Use this book to imagine that moment on a small country road when you round that curve, and there ahead is a barn framed by blue skies, punctuated with the deep colors and the perfect geometry of a quilt block.

Like a crimson dawn rising over green pasture, it'll cause you to say, "Oooo, ahhh!"

– Doug Weaver, Editor

Railroad Crossing

Our first barn is a fitting start, because it's part of one of the best-known and best-organized quilt trails in the country, the Barn Quilts of Sac County.

The trail got its start from the unlikely source of Kevin Peyton, who started the project as a high school student and 4-H'er in 2005. He and others in the county viewed the success of the Adams County, Ohio, project and quickly moved to enlist help from 4-H clubs, area art classes, the Sac County Rural Electric Co-op and others.

Today, Kevin's mom, Sue, keeps the trail's web site updated as the number of barn quilts continues to expand. The trail started with 55 barns; as of this writing, the county's barn quilt committee estimates as many as 130 barn quilts pepper the county.

Needless to say, the trail attracts a lot of tourists. Just ask Betty Frank, whose barn was picked as part of the original 55 "because we're right here on the black-top road."

"The number of visitors has been unreal," she said. "Last weekend on Saturday we had two different groups. Then Sunday we had three. They come from New York, from all over."

Frank Barn
2321 Fox Ave.,
Schaller, Iowa
Painted by:
Odebolt-Arthur School
District art students

It's easy to see why. The Frank's red, green and yellow block, "Railroad Crossing," grabs your eye like its namesake. "Stop, look ..." it beckons.

Betty and Richard, meantime, have a love affair going with their barn, which was built in 1909. "It used to be a milk barn before we purchased it," she said. They acquired the land in 1970 and once used the barn to raise hogs; today the barn is mainly used for storage.

The barn was heavily damaged in a tornado during the 1900s, but its sturdy construction – it features 8-by-8-inch beams with wooden pegs as nails – probably saved it from the storm's final fury.

Betty can recall "vividly" when the quilt block went up – the REC truck with the long boom-arm helping to lift the massive 8-by-8-foot block into position. It truly was a community effort, she said.

And for her, the block holds a special place. Betty's mother used to make quilts ... "for world relief, hundreds of them," she recalls.

Railroad Crossing

Block Size: 12" Finished

Cutting Instructions

From the red fabric, cut
- 10 – 2 1/2" squares

From the black fabric, cut
- 2 – 4 7/8" squares

From the shirting, cut
- 2 – 4 7/8" squares
- 10 – 2 1/2" squares

To Make the Block

You will need to make 4 black/shirting half-square triangles. To make these units, draw a line from corner to corner on the diagonal on the reverse side of the 4 7/8" shirting squares. Place a shirting square atop each black square with right sides facing. Sew 1/4" on either side of the drawn line. Using your rotary cutter, cut along the line. Open each unit and press the seam allowance toward the darkest fabric.

Sew each red square to a white square. Sew two of these units together to make a 4-patch. Make 5.

Sew a 4-patch unit to either side of a half-square triangle unit. Make two rows like this.

Sew a half-square triangle unit to either side of a 4-patch unit.

Sew the three rows together as shown below to complete the block.

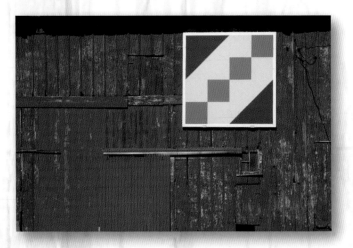

Note: Edie used the traditional nine-patch version of the Railroad Crossing block in the quilt, which is why it differs slightly from the barn quilt.

Railroad Crossing made by Clara Diaz,
Independence, Mo.

Hole in the Barn Door

The Stickrod Corncrib sits on a beautiful Iowa setting of trees, rolling hills and blue skies. And here, it's worth considering the distinction between a barn and a corncrib.

For you city folks, the telltale sign is the structure's exterior walls ... if it has slat-wall siding to allow the air to drift through, chances are it's a crib used for drying grain.

Jack and Marjorie Stickrod purchased this corncrib and the surrounding farm in 1968 from Jack's aunt and uncle, Walter and Dorothy Vogel. Working with the Vogels, he poured a cement floor to update the corncrib.

"It needs a little paint," reported Marjorie, saying the crib was dinged by a hail storm.

But otherwise, it's sitting strong.

This land has some westward-settlement history to it. It was originally purchased from the Iowa Railroad Land Company in 1877, according to the book, *Barn Quilts of Sac County*. Railroads back then were eager to promote the sale of lands along their routes – to prosper from the land sales, of course, but also to build business for the railroad itself.

The corncrib was built by William Aschinger and William (Biddem) Mann much later, in 1954.

Corncribs were first used by Native Americans, and settlers eventually borrowed the idea. The key is those slat walls – usually made of wood, as this one is, but also metal and even cement. Cribs today can be found worldwide.

Stickrod Corncrib
2429 360th St.
Wall Lake, Iowa
Painted by: Viola
Visions/Wall Lake
Bandits 4-H Clubs

The Stickrod's crib was built to store ear corn and small grain in three overhead bins. The building includes an inside elevator. On the roof: a cupola.

This quilt-block design has been published in farm journals, newspapers and other sources through the years under many different names – not unusual with old quilt patterns. You can spot it also as "Monkey Wrench," "Churn Dash," "Pioneer Patch" and "Crow's Nest."

But "Hole in the Barn Door" seems most fitting, corncrib or not.

Hole in the Barn Door

Block Size: 12" Finished

Cutting Directions

From the shirting fabric, cut

- ♦ 2 – 4 7/8" squares
- ♦ 4 – 2 1/2" x 4 1/2" rectangles
- ♦ 1 – 4 1/2" square

From the red fabric, cut

- ♦ 2 – 4 7/8" squares

From the black fabric, cut

- ♦ 4 – 2 1/2" x 4 1/2" rectangles

To Make the Block

You will need to make 4 red/shirting half-square triangles. To make these units, draw a line from corner to corner on the diagonal on the reverse side of the 4 7/8" shirting squares. Pair each shirting square with a red square. Sew 1/4" on either side of the drawn line. Using your rotary cutter, cut along the line. Open each unit and press the seam allowance toward the darkest fabric.

Sew the black and shirting rectangles together. Make 4.

Sew a half-square triangle unit to either end of a rectangle unit. Make 2

Sew the remaining rectangle units to either side of the 4 1/2" square.

Sew the 3 rows together as shown to complete the block.

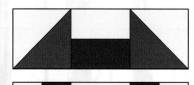

*Hole in the Barn Door made by Brenda Butcher,
Independence, Mo.*

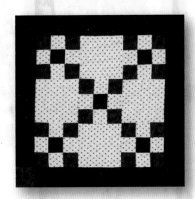

Double Nine-Patch

Carl and Suzanne Lehto's "Double Nine-Patch" is a lesson in self-expression ... an 8-foot-square testimony to family, faith and old-fashioned tractor sales.

First, though, let's explain the setting. This is the first of two barns we've selected in the Old Mission Peninsula area just north of Traverse City, Mich. It's a grass-and-dune region dotted by vineyards and red barns, and graced on both sides by the pure, blue waters of the east and west arms of Traverse Bay.

It's an idyllic setting for the 10 barns on the Barns of Old Mission Quilt Trail.

The Lehtos' barn was built in 1912. They have owned it for the past 39 years, making only occasional repairs such as a new steel roof. All in all, it's stood the test of time just fine.

Given Suzanne's love of quilting, she and Carl jumped at the chance to add a barn quilt to their barn when approached by trail organizer Evelyn Johnson.

And Suzanne, a quilter of 20 years, had just the design in mind – a "Double Nine-Patch" that would allow her and Carl to plug in some symbols important to the Lehtos:

Lehto Barn
15793 Smokey Hollow Road, Traverse City, Mich.
Painted by: Carl and Suzanne Lehto

- A sign of their Christian faith, the Trinity symbol, anchors the high point of the block.
- On the left, the American flag, indicating country.
- On the right, the Finnish flag, symbolizing the Lehtos' Finnish heritage.
- And on the bottom, a symbol of old-fashioned tractor salesmanship – an International Harvester logo to mark the work of Carl's father, who sold IH-made Farmall tractors.

If you don't know the Farmall, it was a best-selling tractor in the '30s and '40s.

Oh, and Carl still has one.

"It's about 60 years old," said Carl. "I use it all around the yard here."

Suzanne loves their quilt block and, in fact, has made an actual 4-foot-square quilt that mimics the one on the barn. She shares her hobby with a small quilting group at church.

Passersby seem to love it, too. They'll snap pictures from the road, and sometimes walk up the drive to get a closer look.

And that's just fine with the Lehtos, who will happily explain the symbols on the block. Or share a tractor story or two.

Double Nine-Patch

Block Size: 12" Finished

Cutting Directions

From the red fabric, cut

- 1 – 1 7/8" strip across the width of the fabric – you must have at least 40" of usable width after trimming off the selvages. Split the strip in half.

From the shirting fabric, cut

- 2 – 1 7/8" strips across the width of the fabric – you must have at least 40" of usable width after trimming off the selvages. Split the strips in half, you will have one strip left over for another project.
- 4 – 4 1/2" squares

From the black fabric, cut

- 1 – 1 7/8" strip across the width of the fabric

To Make the Block

Sew a red strip to either side of a shirting fabric. Cut the strip into 10 - 1 7/8" increments.

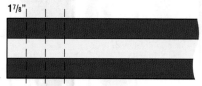

Sew a shirting strip to either side of the black strip. Cut the strip into 5 – 1 7/8" increments.

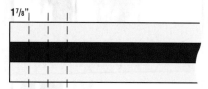

Sew the strips together as shown to make nine-patch units. Make 5.

Sew a 9-patch unit to either side of a shirting square. Make 2 rows like this.

Sew a shirting square to either side of a nine-patch unit. Make 1 row.

Sew the three rows together to complete the block.

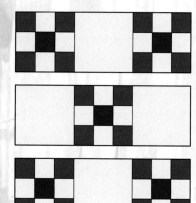

Double Nine-Patch made by Margaret Falen,
Grain Valley, Mo.

Variable Star

This is one tall barn. And there's a story in that.

First, the farm. It's been in the family since August Hanke purchased the land in 1899.

The barn was built by August's son, Edward, a bit later – in the early 1900s. Only there was a small problem. Family history says the lumber yard goofed on Edward's order for barn materials, delivering the wood in lengths much longer than Edward originally wanted.

Rather than cut it all to the right length, Edward decided to just build a taller barn. And so the Hanke Barn was built tall – and even today, seems to tower over the Iowa plains.

Its peak, then, is a perfect setting for the "Variable Star" quilt block – a red, white and blue design popular in the mid '30s. Today you can find many variations of "Variable Star" in quilting literature.

These days, the barn and farm is co-owned by Carole and Robert Hanke and Robert's sister, LaVon Freese.

Hanke Barn
2825 350th St.
Lake View, Iowa
Painted by: Jackson's
4-H of Sac County

The barn has had its rough moments. Like many in Iowa, it has suffered tornado damage. One in particular moved the barn off its foundation; the walls had to be straightened … "to rebalance it," said Carole Hanke.

Today the barn is used for storage but Carole confirms that inside, the 16 milking stanchions are still in place from when the family used to have milk cows. And there are horses' mangers as well.

Given the Hanke Barn's red prominence on the landscape, this seems a fitting point to clear up why so many barns are red in the first place.

According to the *Farmers' Almanac*, it's a tradition that goes back to when farmers would seal their barn walls with linseed oil – before the days of paint and commercial sealer. They also would salt the oil with rust. Rust, always plentiful on the farm, would kill fungi and slow the growth of moss on barn siding. The combination of orange-colored oil and red rust turned the walls a shade of red.

Today, farmers honor that tradition by painting their barns red.

Variable Star

Block Size: 12" Finished

Cutting Directions

From the shirting fabric, cut
- ♦ 4 – 3 1/2" squares
- ♦ 6 – 3 7/8" squares

From the red fabric, cut
- ♦ 4 – 3 7/8" squares

From the black fabric, cut
- ♦ 2 – 3 7/8" squares

To Make the Block

You will need to make 4 black/shirting and 8 red/shirting half-square triangles. To make these units, draw a line from corner to corner on the diagonal on the reverse side of the 3 7/8" shirting squares. Pair each shirting square with the black squares and the red squares. Sew 1/4" on either side of the drawn line. Using your rotary cutter, cut along the line. Open each unit and press the seam allowance toward the darkest fabric.

Sew the squares and half-square triangle units into rows as shown below.

Sew the rows together to complete the block.

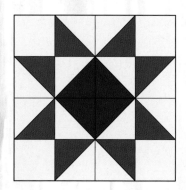

Variable Star made by Edie McGinnis,
Kansas City, Mo.

Wild Goose Chase

Ask a child to sketch a barn, and he'll probably draw a square box with a sharp, inverted "V" for the roof.

Unless he's a dairyman's son. And then he just might draw a "gambrel" roof, a multi-angled design that provides a broader peak at the top and more width on the sides.

Welcome to the Schwaller barn, a fine example in Sac County, Iowa, of the gambrel roof in action. It's no surprise that this barn, which dates to 1950, was used for milking Holstein cows until 1986.

Although it's primarily used as a calving barn now by the owners, Daniel and Linda Schwaller, the original gambrel design made sense. As barn roofs evolved, farmers were seeking ways to add storage to their barns so they could keep their dairy cows inside during the harsh winters. A gambrel roof basically inflated the inside storage space compared with the more traditional "V" of the "gable" roof design.

Mail-order barn makers such as Sears, Roebuck & Co. would eventually take barns another step to a "gothic" roof design – barns with almost a round, inverted "U" shape on top. Storage capacity in those barns was even greater.

This barn features the "Wild Goose Chase" block in brilliant red, purple, blue and green in a background of yellow. The block itself has a variety of names – "Return of the Swallows" and "Dutchman's Puzzle," for example. The triangles of the block, used in this and similar ways, are often portrayed by quilt designers to suggest birds in flight.

Although the barn sits well up on a hill, the Schwallers report that there have been plenty of folks stopping along the highway below to take a look at the quilt block.

Odds are, though, they don't pay much attention to that roofline.

Schwaller Barn
3243 Esther Ave.
Odebolt, Iowa
Painted by: Odebolt-
Arthur art students

Wild Goose Chase

Block Size: 12" Finished

Cutting Directions

From the shirting fabric, cut

♦ 8 – 3 7/8" squares

From the red fabric, cut

♦ 4 – 3 7/8" squares

From the black fabric, cut

♦ 4 – 3 7/8" squares

To Make the Block

You will need to make 8 black/shirting and 8 red/shirting half-square triangles. To make these units, draw a line from corner to corner on the diagonal on the reverse side of the 3 7/8" shirting squares. Pair each shirting square with the black squares and the red squares. Sew 1/4" on either side of the drawn line. Using your rotary cutter, cut along the line. Open each unit and press the seam allowance toward the darkest fabric.

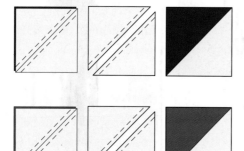

Sew the half-square triangle units into flying geese as shown below. Make 4 of each.

Sew 2 geese together to make one quadrant of the block. Make 2 quadrants like this.

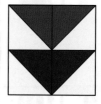

Make 2 quadrants as shown below.

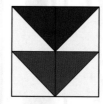

Sew the 4 quadrants together as shown to complete the block.

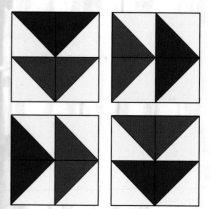

Wild Goose Chase made by Carol Christopher, Independence, Mo.

Hovering Hawks

"Hovering Hawks" is an appropriate name for this quilt block, given its location in the middle of Sac County, Iowa.

After all, Iowa is known as the Hawkeye State, named as a tribute to chief Black Hawk, leader of the Sac Indians who eventually were relocated to Iowa.

Not to mention that hawks routinely soar Iowa's skies.

This barn narrowly missed soaring itself. A tornado ripped through the county in 1970, tossing trees every which way but narrowly missing the house and its outbuildings.

The Schelles had just moved to the new farmhouse when the tornado struck. It took 10 days to burn the three-acre field of debris left in its wake.

Perhaps because of that near miss, Beulah Schelle calls it a good barn ... strong, sturdy, passing the test of time.

Built in 1948, the barn features a "gambrel" roof. And while it's had a range of uses – to shelter cattle, store hay and grain – Beulah and husband James use it today to shelter their horse.

"We used to have sheep, but not any more," she said.

As for the quilt block, "it went up pretty easily," Beulah recalls. "It took a couple of guys and three of my grandsons to put it up."

It was one of the early ones to go up in Sac County; the barn was picked for its proximity to the road.

And that's made it easy to spot. "We have people drive by all the time," Beulah said. "They stop, want to take a picture."

As much as she appreciates her quilt block, Beulah herself isn't a quilter. "At least not yet," she said with a laugh. "But I know a lot of people around here who are. There are some beautiful quilts around here."

Schelle Barn
2359 230th St.
Early, Iowa
Painted by: Schaller-Crestland agriculture students

Hovering Hawks

Block Size: 12" Finished

Cutting Instructions

From the red fabric, cut
- 3 – 3 7/8" squares

From the black fabric, cut
- 2 – 3 7/8" squares

From the shirting, cut
- 5 – 3 7/8" squares
- 6 – 3 1/2" squares

To Make the Block

You will need to make 6 red/shirting and 4 black/shirting half-square triangles. To make these units, draw a line from corner to corner on the diagonal on the reverse side of the 3 7/8" shirting squares. Place a shirting square atop each red square and each black square with right sides facing. Sew 1/4" on either side of the drawn line. Using your rotary cutter, cut along the line. Open each unit and press the seam allowance toward the darkest fabric.

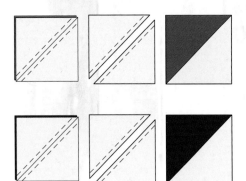

Sew the squares and half-square triangles into rows as shown below.

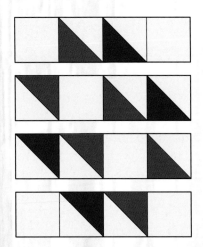

Sew the rows together to complete the block.

Hovering Hawks made by Edie McGinnis,
Kansas City, Mo.

Corn and Beans

Here's our second corncrib of the bunch and, oh my, are there some interesting stories with this one – about a scary upstairs, a giant rock and a '37 Plymouth.

First, the farm itself. Dean Larson's family moved to the farm when Dean was just six years old, in 1954. The move to the farm's big farmhouse was quite a change from where the Larsons lived before – a small house in the nearby area of Sherbonville.

"Dean got lost upstairs the first day, it was so much bigger," said Carol Larson. And Dean's sisters, being sisters, didn't bother to help the panicked Dean find his way out.

Then there's a rickety old farmhouse just in front of the corncrib. "That house wasn't even on the abstract" when the family acquired the farm, Carol said. So its history is a mystery.

There's a giant rock in front of it, but that's easily explained: The Larsons dragged it from the field to rest atop a time capsule buried on Dean's 50th birthday. The plan was to uncover it on Dean's 60th birthday, which they did. But they left the rock there.

As for the worn-out farmhouse, the Larsons have held on to it because of what's inside ...a '38 Plymouth. Or more specifically, the car's backseat.

The story goes that Dean's father was a dairy farmer. Dean's mother was planning on Dean being born in the nearby hospital. But when the time came for Dean to arrive, all was set ... except, as any good dairy farmer knows, cows can't necessarily wait to be milked.

"His dad just wasn't done milking yet," explained Carol.

So Dad furiously milked, then they jumped in the car, roared to the hospital and ... didn't quite make it.

"He was born in the backseat," Carol said.

Finally, there's the corncrib itself. Dean and Carol have framed the quilt block with a wagon wheel, picket fence and birdhouse.

Larson Corncrib
10067 E. 7000N Road,
Grant Park, Ill.
Painted by: Kankakee
County Extension

The block is appropriately named "Corn and Beans." At the time of these photos, the corncrib was bordered on the east by corn. Because of crop-rotation techniques, the field next year will feature soybeans. The next year, corn, then beans, then corn ....

You get the idea.

"We looked through pattern after pattern," Carol said. "We thought, 'That has to be the one!'"

Carol says folks are welcome to visit. "It's neat to see them stop and take pictures."

If you do, ask for a story or two.

Corn and Beans

Block Size: 12" Finished

Cutting Directions

From the shirting fabric, cut

- 3 – 4 7/8" squares – Cut each square from corner to corner once on the diagonal.
- 10 – 2 7/8" squares – Cut 4 squares from corner to corner once on the diagonal.

From the red fabric, cut

- 1 – 4 7/8" squares – Cut each square from corner to corner once on the diagonal.
- 4 – 2 7/8" squares – Cut each square from corner to corner once on the diagonal.

From the black fabric, cut

- 6 – 2 7/8" squares

To Make the Block

You will need to make 12 black/shirting half-square triangles. To make these units, draw a line from corner to corner on the diagonal on the reverse side of the 2 7/8" shirting squares. Pair each shirting square with a black square. Sew 1/4" on either side of the drawn line. Using your rotary cutter, cut along the line. Open each unit and press the seam allowance toward the darkest fabric.

Sew 2 black and shirting half-square triangles together as shown to make a flying geese unit. Make 4 and set aside.

Sew the 2 large red triangles to 2 large shirting triangles as shown to make the center of the block.

Sew a small shirting triangle to either side of a black/shirting half-square triangle. Make 4 and sew each to the center of the block.

Sew a red triangle to either end of the flying geese units. Make 4 and sew each to the center of the block as shown

Sew a large shirting triangle to each corner as shown to complete the block.

Corn and Beans made by Clara Diaz,
Independence, Mo.

Star and Four-Patch

This is the second barn quilt from the beautiful Old Mission Peninsula in northern Michigan. And this one is graced by a horse ... and a mischievous one at that! But more on that in a bit.

First, this barn's a beaut. It was built on a hillside in 1870 by homesteader Julius Marshall, and it remained in the Marshall family for many years. Glen and Rebecca Chown acquired the farm in 1995.

But the barn definitely needed work, recalls Rebecca. An old attached shed, not part of the original construction, was falling down and pulling much of the barn with it. So the Chowns secured the structure, put in new hayloft steps and made a few other improvements. They use it today for hay and general storage.

The barn's quilt block, meanwhile, ties back to Rebecca's personal history. "We were trying to think up a pattern that had significance to the family," Rebecca said. "My great-grandmother was a quilter, and my mom inherited her quilts."

So Rebecca and mom pored through the collection searching for the ideal pattern, finally settling on a quilt featuring the "Star and Four-Patch." The

Chown Barn
2877 Old Mission Road
Traverse City, Mich.
Painted by: Rebecca Chown

colors of that particular quilt block weren't best for the barn, though – "It was pink!" said Rebecca – so they found inspiration in another of great-grandmother's quilts.

The block's links to family mean a lot to the Chowns. "We've tried to preserve many traditions (on the farm), and that's one we cherish," Rebecca said.

Owning a horse, meanwhile, is one tradition the Chowns have now decided to skip. The horse in the photo, Doll, "has a temper ... a vicious streak," Rebecca reported. And although the Chowns tried, they just couldn't get their Doll to warm up to the family, including the kids.

"It's a very naughty horse," Rebecca said.

So Doll is gone, under new ownership ... "and we wish her well."

Which isn't to say the meadow is horse-free. "We're boarding other horses now," said Rebecca.

They're just nicer ones.

Star and Four-Patch

Block Size: 12" Finished

Cutting Instructions

From the shirting fabric, cut

- ♦ 8 – 2 1/2" squares
- ♦ 4 – 2 1/2" x 4 1/2" rectangles
- ♦ 4 – 2 7/8" squares

From the red fabric, cut

- ♦ 8 – 2 1/2" squares

From the black fabric, cut

- ♦ 1 – 4 1/2" square
- ♦ 4 – 2 7/8" squares

To Make the Block

You will need to make 8 black/shirting half-square triangles. To make these units, draw a line from corner to corner on the diagonal on the reverse side of the 2 7/8" shirting squares. Pair each shirting square with a black square. Sew 1/4" on either side of the drawn line. Using your rotary cutter, cut along the line. Open each unit and press the seam allowance toward the darkest fabric.

Sew the half-square triangles together as shown below to make flying geese. Make 4 geese.

Stitch a shirting rectangle to each flying geese unit. Make 4.

Sew the 2 1/2" red and shirting squares together into 4-patch units. Make 4.

Sew a four patch unit to either side of a flying geese unit. Make two rows like this.

Sew a flying geese unit to either side of the black 4 1/2" square.

Sew the three rows together as shown to complete the block.

*Star and Four-Patch made by Margaret Falen,
Grain Valley, Mo.*

Mosaic

As folks close to college sports know, pride in state universities sometimes runs strongest in farm communities.

After all, many universities were built upon agriculture itself, and they continue to share "best-of-class" techniques with their states' farmers.

So perhaps it's not surprising to find college loyalty, agricultural success and a rich farm-family tradition combining in a huge way at this farm just outside Kankakee, Ill., our second on the Kankakee Barn Trail.

The Moritz barn sits on the west side of the Kankakee County area, which straddles Interstate 57 as it snakes its way from Illinois' most southern tip to Chicago on the north.

The college connection to the barn is clear to any University of Illinois grad: This "Mosaic" barn-quilt pattern sports the school's blue and orange colors of the Fighting Illini.

"My oldest two sons graduated from the University of Illinois, the second oldest just in May," explains Kristi Moritz, who with her husband Phillip operate the farm. Kristi picked the Mosaic pattern because she thought it and the colors would look striking against the barn's white exterior.

Moritz Barn
19081 W. 5500S Road
Buckingham, Ill.
Painted by: Kankakee
County Extension

Only later did friends suggest the pattern had a Native American feel to it, reflecting the Illini tribe that once roamed most of Illinois.

Although Kristi is not a quilter, she has a very good friend who quilts.

"She tries to get me to do it ... they have a sewing group that meets, and it's a popular thing to do during the winter months."

By the way, those sons are sticking close to agriculture ... both are working now in ag-related companies.

And that gets us to the second half of the Illinois connection. The barn, built by the family in 1949, has housed more than its share of winners at the Illinois State Fair in Springfield. Kristi's father and the two oldest sons have won the prestigious Grand Champion Steer or Bull awards, for example, and numerous other champion steers and hogs were raised in the barn during the family's three generations.

These days, the focus is just on hogs.

"Our youngest son is in 4-H; he has his show hogs out there," said Kristi.

Sounds like a winner.

Mosaic

Block Size: 12" Finished

Cutting Instructions

From the red fabric, cut

- ♦ 2 – 4 7/8" squares
- ♦ 1 – 3 3/8" square

From the black fabric, cut

- ♦ 4 – 5 1/4" squares

From the shirting, cut

- ♦ 2 – 4 7/8" squares
- ♦ 4 – 5 1/4" squares
- ♦ 2 – 2 7/8" squares – cut each square from corner to corner once on the diagonal.

To Make the Block

You will need to make 4 red/shirting half-square triangles. To make these units, draw a line from corner to corner on the diagonal on the reverse side of the 4 7/8" shirting squares. Place a shirting square atop a red square with right sides facing. Sew 1/4" on either side of the drawn line. Using your rotary cutter, cut along the line. Open each unit and press the seam allowance toward the darkest fabric.

You will also need to make 4 black/shirting hour-glass blocks. Draw a line from corner to corner on the reverse side of the 5 1/4" shirting squares. Place a shirting square atop a black square with right sides facing. Sew 1/4" on either side of the drawn line. Cut along the drawn line, open each unit and press toward the black fabric. You now have half-square triangles.

Place two half-square triangle blocks together with right sides facing. Snug the seam lines up against each other. Draw a line from corner to

corner on the reverse side of the half-square triangle blocks and sew 1/4" on either side of the drawn line. Cut along the drawn line, open and press.

Make the center of the block by sewing a 2 7/8" shirting triangle to opposing sides of the red square.

Now sew the remaining triangles to the square.

Sew a red/shirting half-square triangle to either side of an hour glass unit. Make two rows like this.

Sew an hour glass unit to either side of the center square.

Sew the three rows together to complete the block.

*Mosaic made by Brenda Butcher,
Independence, Mo.*

Putting It All Together

Cutting Instructions

From the black fabric, cut

- ♦ 12 – 2 1/2" x 12 1/2" strips
- ♦ 2 – 2 1/2" x 40 1/2" strips
- ♦ 2 – 2 1/2" x 44 1/2" strips (you may have to piece this if your fabric isn't wide enough)
- ♦ 4 – 4 1/2" squares

From the red fabric, cut

- ♦ 4 – 2 1/2" squares
- ♦ 4 – 4 1/2" x 44 1/2" strips for the outer border (piece if necessary)

Sew a sashing strip to the right side of block 1. Add block 2 and sew a sashing strip to the right side. Add block 3, completing the top row.

Refer to the diagram below and sew the rows of blocks and sashing together.

Make 2 rows of horizontal sashing. Sew a red square to one end of a black sashing strip. Add another sashing strip, a red square and a black sashing strip. Make 2 strips like the one shown below.

Sew the block rows and sashing rows together. Refer to the diagram below if necessary.

The center of the quilt should measure 40 1/2" square at this point. If it doesn't, adjust your border strips accordingly. Sew a 2 1/2" x 40 1/2" black border strip to the sides of the quilt.

Sew a 2 1/2" x 44 1/2" black border strip to the top and bottom of the quilt.

Add the next border by sewing a 4 1/2" x 44 1/2" red strip to both sides of the quilt.

Sew a black 4 1/2" square to both ends of the remaining red strips. Sew one strip to the top of the quilt and one to the bottom.

Layer the quilt with batting and backing and bind.

Barn Quilt Resources

Here is a list of web sites across the country with information on local barn trails.

The first group includes sites of general interest – blogs that track trends in barn quilts.

The second group includes the three barn trails we visited to create this book.

The third group is a state-by-state listing of barn trails whose organizers have created web sites.

Some caveats: Some barn trails exist out there but their organizers have not yet set up web sites. Because of research constraints, we could not list all barn trails ... only those with web sites. Also, we listed only those web sites that were functioning when this book was published. Finally, our apologies if we missed your web site! The list is ever-changing as new barn trails come on line.

General Sites

Barn Quilts and the American Trail Blog: http://americanquilttrail.blogspot.com/

Barn Quilt Memories Blog: http://barnquiltmemories.blogspot.com/

American Quilt Barns: http://www.americanquiltbarns.com/

Barn Trails Featured in this Book

Barns of Old Mission, Traverse City, Mich.: http://www.barnsofoldmission.com/

Barn Quilts of Kankakee County, Ill.: http://web.extension.illinois.edu/kankakee/barn/index.html

Barn Quilts of Sac County, Iowa: http://www.barnquilts.com/

State by State Listing

Arkansas

Randolph County: http://www.5rhp.org/downloads/QuiltBooklet.pdf

California

Lake County: http://www.pearfestival.com/quilts.asp

Colorado

Morgan County: http://barnquilting.ning.com/profile/MCArtsCouncil

Georgia

Cobb County: http://southernquilttrail.com/

Illinois

Kankakee County: http://web.extension.illinois.edu/kankakee/barn/index.html

McHenry County: http://www.mchsonline.org/quilted_barn_program

Indiana

Elkhart County: http://www.amishcountry.org/quiltgardens/

Marshall County: http://marshallcountytourism.org/

Iowa

Buchanan County: http://www.heartlandacresusa.com/page.php?page=45

Buena Vista County: http://www.bvbarnquilts.com/

Butler County: http://www.butlercountyiowa.com/barnquilts.html

Clay County: http://travelclaycountyiowa.com/barn_quilts.htm

Fayette County: http://www.wadenaiowa.com/barnquilts.htm

Green County: http://www.greenecountyiowadevelopment.org/gcdc-barnquilts.php

Grundy County: http://www.grundycountyia.com/Quilt_Website/Barn_Quilt_Info.htm

Hamilton County, Iowa: http://develop.hamiltoncountyiowa.com/html/barn_quilts.html

Hancock County: http://www.northiowanews.com/articles/2007/09/05/britt_news/news04.txt

Humboldt County: http://www.humboldtcountybarnquilts.com/

Lewis (town of): http://www.cityoflewis.com/default.asp?page=Barn%20Quilts

O'Brien County: http://www.obriencounty.com/tourism/oc_bq_index.html

Plymouth County: http://www.extension.iastate.edu/plymouth/news/barn.htm

Sac County: http://www.barnquilts.com/

Washington County: http://www.barnquiltsiowa.com/

Kentucky

Kentucky Quilt Trails: http://www.kentuckyquilttrail.org/

Kentucky Quilt Trail: http://www.kyheritagequilttrail.com/

Bath, Carter, Elliott, Greenup, Menifee, Montgomery, Morgan and Rowan counties: http://www.kentuckyquilttrail.org/squarepages/trailshome.html

Bracken County: http://home.windstream.net/augustaky/

Breckinridge County: http://www.visitbreckinridgecountyky.com/index.php?mact=News,cntnt01,detail,0&cntnt01articleid=7&cntnt01origid=15&cntnt01returnid=63

Campbell County: http://cckyquilts.wordpress.com/

Cirttenden, Livingston, Lyon, Caldwell, Trigg, Christian, Hopkins, Muhlenberg and Todd counties: http://kentuckyquiltline.com/index.html

Gallatin County: http://ces.ca.uky.edu/gallatin/barnquiltsquare

Georgetown County: http://www.georgetownky.com/barnquilt_web_pg/indexquilt2.html

Grayson County: http://www.graysoncountytourism.com/quilts.htm

Harrison County: http://www.harrisoncountybarnquilts.com/

Hart County: http://ces.ca.uky.edu/hart/node/69

Henry County: http://www.henrycountyky.com/extension/barnquilts.htm

Hickman County: http://hickmancoquilttrail.wordpress.com/

Jessamine County: http://kentuckyquilttrail-jessaminecounty.com/

Lewis County: http://www.visitlewiscountyky.com/quilttrail/quilttrailhome.html

Madison County: http://ces3.ca.uky.edu/madisonquilttrail/trail.html

Marion County: http://www.visitlebanonky.com/attractions/quilts.htm

Ohio County: http://ces.ca.uky.edu/ohio/barnquilttrail

Owen County: http://owencountyquilttrail.com/home.html

Rowan County: http://rcquilttrail.tripod.com/

Scott County: http://www.georgetownky.com/barnquilt_web_pg/indexquilt2.html

Washington County: http://ces.ca.uky.edu/washington-files/WASHINGTONCOUNTY_BARN_QUILT_TRAIL.pdf

Maryland

Garrett County: http://www.garrettbarnquilts.org/

Michigan

Alcona County: http://alconaquilttrail.com/

Grand Traverse County: http://www.barnsofoldmission.com/

Minnesota

Houston County: http://www.caledoniamn.gov/index.asp?Type=B_BASIC&SEC={EEEC671F-67D1-4764-95B4-BB3DFEBF8270}

Missouri

Barn Quilts of Boonslick: http://www.sedaliademocrat.com/articles/boonslick-18059-together-council.html

Nebraska

Cass County: http://embarn.freehostia.com/index.html

New Jersey

Middlesex County: http://www.njbarnquilts.com/middlesexcoquilts.html

Sussex County: http://www.njbarnquilts.com/sussexcoquilts.html

Warren County: http://www.njbarnquilts.com/warrencoquilts.html

New York

Neversink County: http://www.townofneversink.org/barn_quilts.html

Orleans County: http://www.countrybarnquilttrail.com/

North Carolina

Western North Carolina: http://www.quilttrailswnc.org/

Alexander County: http://www.hiddenitecenter.com/alexupdate.htm

Ashe County: http://www.ashecountyarts.org/

Avery County: http://www.averycountyartscouncil.org/pages/avery_quilt_trail.html

Macon County: http://www.maconcountyquilttrail.org/

Madison County: http://www.madisoncountyarts.com/mcac/QUILTS.CFM

McDowell County: http://mcdowellquilttrail.org/

Watauga County: http://www.watauga-arts.org/pages/barn.html

Wilkes County: http://www.cacwilkes.org/2008/barn_quilts.htm

Yadkin County: http://www.shacktownnc.com/YadkinValleyQuiltTrail.php

Ohio

Ohio Quilt Barns: http://www.ohiobarns.com/index.html

Athens County: http://www.athensohio.com/whattodo/index.php?page=25&item=76

Brown County: http://www.browncountytourism.com/

Clinton County: http://www.ccbarnquilts.com/

Fayette, Highland and Ross counties: http://www.greenfieldhistoricalsociety.org/ghs-quilt-barn-trail.html

Harrison County: http://bender.frognet.net/~harrisoncic/community/quiltbarn.htm

Miami County: http://www.visitmiamicounty.org/barnquilts.html

Pike County: http://www.piketravel.com/cvb-quilt-trail.html

Vinton County: http://www.vintoncountytravel.com/quilt_barns.htm

Oregon

Tillamook County: http://www.latimerquiltandtextile.com/html/tillamook_county_quilt_trail.html

Pennsylvania

Wyalusing (city of): http://www.wyalusing.net/barnquilt/

South Carolina

Oconee County: http://www.oconeeheritagequilttrail.com/Oconee%20Heritage%20Quilt%20Trail.html

Tennessee

Quilt Trail of Northeast Tennessee: http://216.122.45.15/quilttrail/index.htm

Anderson County: http://www.vacationaqt.com/trail/county/anderson-tn.htm

Blount County: http://www.vacationaqt.com/trail/county/blount-tn.htm

Carter County: http://www.vacationaqt.com/trail/county/carter-tn.htm

Claiborne County: http://www.vacationaqt.com/trail/county/claiborne-tn.htm

Cocke County: http://www.vacationaqt.com/trail/county/cocke-tn.htm

Grainger County: http://www.vacationaqt.com/trail/county/grainger-tn.htm

Greene County: http://www.vacationaqt.com/trail/county/greene-tn.htm

Hamblen County: http://www.vacationaqt.com/trail/county/hamblen-tn.htm

Hancock County: http://www.vacationaqt.com/trail/county/hancock-tn.htm

Hawkins County: http://www.vacationaqt.com/trail/county/hawkins-tn.htm

Houston County: http://www.houstoncochamber.com/news.php?viewStory=377

Jefferson County: http://jeffersoncountyvacation.com/historical-attractions/smoky-mountain-quilt-trail/

Johnson County: http://www.vacationaqt.com/trail/county/johnson-tn.htm

Knox County: http://www.vacationaqt.com/trail/county/knox-tn.htm

Monroe County: http://www.vacationaqt.com/trail/county/monroe-tn.htm

Montgomery County: http://www.vacationaqt.com/trail/county/montgomery-tn.htm

Sevier County: http://www.vacationaqt.com/trail/county/sevier-tn.htm

Sullivan County: http://www.vacationaqt.com/trail/county/sullivan-tn.htm

Unicoi County: http://www.vacationaqt.com/trail/county/unicoi-tn.htm

Union County: http://www.vacationaqt.com/trail/county/union-tn.htm

Washington County: http://www.vacationaqt.com/trail/county/washington-tn.htm

Texas

Terry County: http://www.terrycountyquilts.com/

Virginia

Lee County: http://www.vacationaqt.com/trail/county/lee-va.htm

West Virginia

Kentucky-Ohio-West Virginia trail: http://www.ohiobarns.com/otherbarns/quilt/quiltbarns.html

Wisconsin

Green County: http://www.greencountybarnquilts.com/

Kewaunee County: http://agriculturalheritage.org/barnquilts/

Lafayette County: http://www.uwex.edu/CES/cty/lafayette/documents/Brochure.pdf

Racine County: http://www.quiltsonbarns.com/

Rock County: http://rock.uwex.edu/BarnQuiltsofRockCountyWIsconsin.html

Walworth County: http://walworth.uwex.edu/ag/barnquilts.html